Future of Work:
The Complete Blueprint

Future of Work:

The Complete Blueprint

Reema Nakra

Contents

**Rewriting the Rules of the Workplace and
Future Talent Success Stories**

PREFACE

In the last five years, there has been a significant rise in the skill requirements of work, due to swift technological changes and enhancing global competition. This necessitates quick improvements in higher education to build young people with the higher skills needed for the coming century. Until the beginning of 2020, humans were far superior at any work that depends on imagination, entrepreneurialism, leadership abilities and emotional intelligence. ⍰

A lot of people who are apprehensive about the future of jobs don't know what skills to learn or practise. To add woes, the lockdown across the world necessitated due to the Covid-19 has curtailed preparation time for companies. Businesses are compelled to find new approaches and new technology to survive.

Reema Nakra, the Founder of Delhi-based Talent Search Management Consulting explores and unravels the factors that will be influencing how people work and foresees what companies require to survive and thrive in the future. Her ideas and guiding principles will reassure you to challenge out-dated, traditional beliefs and practices.

Skilled in a myriad of HR functionalities, Reema Nakra discusses in her book titled 'Future of Work:- The Complete Blueprint' on the social and technological trends that impact the future workplace.

The well-researched book contains 10 chapters and lists the prevailing practices adopted in the HR, ways of measuring and retaining the talent, as well as ways of empowering individuals to shape their careers and allow them to take ownership of their constant learning and development.

Hopefully, this reading list she has put together will serve as a blueprint for organizations as it guides them on shaping talent management strategies vis-à-vis resourcing, employee engagement, building future talent pools and reward programs.

Since its establishment in 2019, TSMC, under the able leadership of Reema, is passionately committed to working with a sense of trust and creating good business relationships by maintaining a positive attitude and accountability.

TSMC is ably backed by professionals who have built a solid reputation in engaging with a broad spectrum of businesses namely IT, Health care and Pharma, FMCG, Consumer Durables, Automotive, Engineering, Retail, Telecom etc, in providing end-to-end flexible recruitment solutions, including contract, temporary and regular hire options. ⍰

With an exclusive focus on supporting the talent development profession, TSMC-sponsored Learning & Development Training help employees in getting ready for a job. ⍰

Chapter-1

The New Future of Work in a Post-pandemic World

Workplaces undergo frantic alterations.

The unexpected outbreak of the pandemic has given a little time for organizations to prepare future strategies. Still, companies were able to overcome potential infrastructure problems to enhance the speed of decision making, while boosting productivity, using technology and data in fresh ways, and speeding up the scope and scale of innovation.

Businesses entered the digital workplace, swiftly adjusting to new tools and new ways of working. While the first few weeks had been tremendously demanding, with companies' primary focus on mobilizing their people to Work at Home, most of them have now settled into the so-called "New Normal", celebrating successes and learning from failures. ▨

With the toughest period behind us, it's time to focus our attention on the future of work in the post-pandemic world. It is widely assumed that many of the changes triggered by the situation will be either irreversible or long-lasting, with flexibility and digitization among the top future of work trends in contemplation. ⏎

The future of work creative work and innovation are within our reach

Pic Source: trainingjournal.com

Deloitte, one of the world's top management consultancies, throwing light on the trends in HR, in its 2017 report, said that the "future of work" will possibly gain pace in the next half-decade. This is simply a task of where we are in the growth of technology. Fifty years after the invention of Moore's law, processing and computing power continue to rise exponentially, driving growth in robotics machine learning. Cognitive tools to expand, and in some cases emerge as substitutes, knowledge work will continue to witness an upward trend and become extensively deployed and adopted. It will not be a startling revelation if the future of work, workforce, and work station issues come to dictate the concerns and agenda of HR and business leaders in the near future. This challenge needs major cross-functional consideration, effort, and cooperation.

Source: www2.deloitte.com

How companies will respond to the COVID-19?

Companies are turning towards an emphasis on business outcomes, then on hours being spent on the system. In the post-pandemic, there is a paradigm shift required at the leadership level to lend stability and normalcy in terms of how people communicate with each other, where they work, and the manner they travel. There will be ever increased collaboration as people search for more rewarding jobs and consider their work as part of a larger movement towards social good.

Managing Social Welfare Remotely

This compels leaders to consider the welfare of employees in different ways. This suggests understanding how the pandemic and associated quarantine rules affect the mental, physical and financial wellbeing of working staff. Millions of employees passed through economic hardship during the time of the pandemic, as they succeeded in managing their work role with needs of home-schooling or posing as caregivers for relatives. Burnout becomes a challenge for one year or more after the COVID ends, as working staff will find it tough to cope with new normal, specifically during the periods where workplaces changed from office atmosphere to home. Companies should set their sights on increasing their mental health service offerings and make resources available to enable employees to handle stress and change to changing conditions. ▨

In the post-pandemic scenario, many businesses may have to let workers work remotely, either in a regular or part-time capacity. For instance, the leading social media marketing agencies like Twitter and Square announced a permanent remote-work policy for a majority of workers. There' societal, environmental, ecological, and productivity advantages to such a shift, but there are some pitfalls too. The main issue is less social interaction. In-office workers mingle with each other socially for major parts of the average day. Work friendships are important and often exist for the long term and moving these interactions to virtual video conferencing will have a significant impact. Businesses do not wish to miss the advantages of personal interaction such as brainstorming sessions and feelings of "belonging" that transform into enhanced employee performance. Apart from this, there are productivity trade-offs too. Rather than settling an issue with a 30-second chat, remote employees might opt for email communications that can wrap tone and intent or planning a meaningless 15-minute Zoom.

The bigger shift to working remotely and leveraging video and other teamwork tools will also merge into changing the manner business people travel and link with partners and customers.

Conclusion: The future of work in the post-pandemic scenario will stay strong, as it has for the last 100 years. In the coming future, we all will be witnessing the development of a hybrid approach, comprising remote workers, usage of reduced spaces for workspaces, and curtailed business travel, all resulting in enhanced work-life balances for millions of workers.

*****

Chapter 2

The Rise of Co-working Spaces Across the Global Spectrum

The business concept of co-working spaces is fast gaining popularity across the world, discontinuing stereotypical and out-dated practices of office establishments.

With technology mobilizing the workforce and remote work becoming more common, demand for workspace is increasing.

In the last two decades, the modern office has experienced countless evolutions. The initial period of 2000 experienced the death of cubicle farms and the advent of open floor plans. And in 2015, and 2015 marked waves of ping pong and foosball tables to offices in all places. While office trends occur and disappear, one thing that does not bring in any variation is the effect that the office environment has on employee health and welfare.

A worth workspace design results in a less traumatic and increased productive atmosphere. It is important that employers take into consideration their employees' physical work atmosphere. In order to perform to their potential, workers must feel relaxed and secure in their physical work environments.

Co-space Facts

There are roughly 35,000 flexible workspaces throughout the world, representing 521 million square feet of flexible space. The global market size of flexible workspaces is valued at $26 billion.

Co-working and Company Culture

The culture of a company, combined with its corporate plan, contributes to greater commitment, productivity and a healthy workforce. Thus, exposure to a vibrant culture of the workplace and many ways to engage the employees is also one of the profitable ways of being a part of a shared workplace.

Gearing up for re-entry

Gone are the times when the working class had the luxury of functioning within the 9-5 timeframe. In current times, the corporate world finds its identity in the form of start-ups, flexible working hours and the ease of space. This, in turn, has transformed the manner we work, including our office space. Amid this scenario, co-working has come to light as one of the quickest-growing trends in the work environment.

This is further corroborated by a JLL Report that revealed that the share of co-working in the whole office leasing increased from 8 per cent in 2018 to 12 per cent in the quarter of 2019. ⬚

How did the Co-working spaces evolve?

In the beginning, the popularity of these flexible workspaces was confined to just freelance professionals and start-ups. In the later stages, they have become a crucial part of the corporate office structure. Realizing it has scores of benefits, many people in the corporate circles have embraced the change. Not only do these result in an enabling environment that facilitates professionals to channel their imagination, and lift productivity, but it also enables one to join likeminded and different professionals, from a selected group of industries. It is no surprise that the co-working section is today a flourishing real estate activity for landlords and plays an important part in the strategy to draw occupiers.

Co-working facilitates enhancement in productivity and builds creativity too

Research demonstrates that being encircled by likeminded persons can boost one's productivity considerably. Co-working companies provide facility management that allows users to bring down their operational costs and enhance productivity. Introducing Artificial Intelligence in co-working habitats permits smart desks that workers can use to control lights and heating. As this technology evolves, it will drive the co-working revolution in the future.

Pic: A dedicated young men and women somehow managing to beat the odds in the COVID scenario to be able to deliver the best.

Source: https://www.indiaaccelerator.co

Co-working spaces lower start-up operating costs

Any commercial start-up, during its incubation period, has to cope with a tough situation to build sales thus covering costs that went into the market phase in time. During such periods, there is a high threat of closing down the business due to the company's failed strategy or less or lack of productivity.

Below are some of the best ways that can be of great help to a shared working space, particularly for start-ups, costing them less in their first stage of establishment:

- Rent problems: The principal benefit of this concept is rental cost-efficiency. Renting the entire co-working space will not be a burden on individual or organizations.

  All the companies that rent dedicated office spaces and workstations bear the cost of the entire space together. This saves a great deal of money that can be used for other constructive purposes.

- Cheap pricing: A co-working space is a perfect choice for a start-up or business that is not in a position to spend money on huge rental or upfront office space.

The sharing spaces offer them with an economical alternative option. This is possible since the pricing structure is quite flexible for these spaces.

- <u>Overall expenditure is less:</u> A shared space, to a large extent, not only adds to the knowledge gained by the candidate but helps him place his office in a prime area with reduced cost to pay for the same. Reducing unnecessary expenditure means you will be able to enhance other facilities in co-working space, like scanning machines, sound-proof areas, and conference rooms so on.

- <u>Expenditure in separate workplaces</u>:
  1. Power supply
  2. Decorations and Furniture
  3. Insurance
  4. Manager handling work
  5. Internet Services
  6. Caretaker
  7. Security

Travel time to off will be reduced if we relook into workspaces ☐

The number of people wishing to live near their workplaces is on the rise and "walk to work" is a trend that is fast gaining momentum in metro cities as it saves productive man-hours rather than losing precious time to traffic congestion for long hours while travelling to work. Given multiple locations, inter-city and as well as intra-city, co-working spaces are the right solution to cut down commuting time and offer both personal and business benefits. Companies are more employee-friendly policies and exploring the possibility of encouraging workers to 'work from home'.

HR Plays a Stellar role in Ensuring a Successful Co-working Space

In today's competitive hiring environment, HR has many changes to address, such as attracting and retaining the right kind of talent and creating a work environment that motivates and engages them.

They will have to come up with new strategies to do so, by leaving behind the conventional retention policies and moving on the current, more competitive methods to keep the workers satisfied at work.

There are several reasons for HR managers to find co-working spaces as a hidden tool for hiring and retaining workers.

Successful and More Productive Employees

The primary objective of any recruitment agency/ human resources department is to spot and attract the most quailed workers for the job.

Employees with high morale who enjoy what they are performing and the atmosphere in which they're employed are more likely to remain on the job for a long period of time.

Expanded Competencies

Co-working spaces will also help HR managers to broaden the skill set and efficiency of work when at work, which is something all workers can enjoy. It is due to the diverse community of people who often work in co-working spaces, all from entrepreneurs, freelancers, designers and lawyers.

Widened Social Networks

Competent HR Managers should endeavour to nurture a social environment for the working staff where everyone can feel like they belong.

Many surveys have concluded that when working in a co-working space, workers tend to be more social and happier in turn when engaged at work in a co-working space.

Enhanced Flexibility at work

As a large number of co-working spaces provide the round-the-clock access, by using these flexible-hour spaces, HR can give employees greater control over their workday and hours.

Co-working spaces effectively help HR compensate for more workers who may not be able to work during the traditional 9-5 schedule.

Conclusion: To sum up, it can be said that Co-working spaces are a compelling thing in the future. This model works to the advantage of everyone given the beginning of the work transformation. In the next 5 years, as people's lifestyle changes, technology advancements occur at a quicker pace, increasing commuting time to offices and the office-going employees will be placed at the heart of all solutions to office space. Also, a large number of entrepreneurs are keen to be a part of participative spaces since experience becomes valuable only when it is shared.

By allowing employees to work in shared workspaces, HR will enable them to be more productive. At the same time, workers are presented with opportunities to acquire new skills, build new networks and strike a better balance between life and work. ⍰

*****

Chapter-3

How HR with Technology will change the future of work?

The Ever Enhancing Role Technology Plays in Human Resources Management

HRD is a crucial part of any corporate office environment. Whether it's recruiting new employees, training, or ensuring compliance with local labour laws, HR processes are a vital part of every business. The enthusiastic workers who make up HR must have a propensity not only to manage the human element (i.e. handling employee issues) but also to use associate technology, including a variety of software solutions for human resources.

The most successful HR personnel must have a varied skillset and flexibility aptitude that allows them to cope with many challenges of their head-on roles. Of course, it is not just the dedicated staff who make up HR. Companies need to provide their HR departments with the tools they require to get the job finished. More and more it means

17

executing HR management programs as well as HR analytics software.

Organizations are placing greater demands on their HR departments than ever before, expecting them not only to manage the hiring, onboarding and exiting processes of employees (not to mention the creation of a strong and supportive corporate culture in the meantime) but also to track their activities, productivity and the general mood of the office to suggest improvements. They need appropriate technology for these tasks. ⏸

Critical Technological Considerations for HR Services

In the near future, the below-mentioned are some of the technological necessities that might be needed by HR to provide appropriate labour management services. ⏸

Employee Management Software

Employee management is the core part of every HR solution. High-end HR software will enable organizations to plan their workforce according to workload demands. This puts an end to double-entry mistakes and multiple updates. ⏸

This software is designed to manage the headcount, set up a schedule, allocate compensation, and establish an HR strategy within the allocated budget. Further, it can make a significant difference in terms of communication, handling projects, and tracking worker contributions for praise, promotions, raise in pay, and bonuses etc. When all these things are properly managed, employee engagement enhances and productivity also increases.

Integrated Management Systems

Within the corporate structure, HR is increasingly called upon to work with other departments. Although they have always shared work responsibilities with the payroll department, they might now be required to share information and resources, for instance, with the legal department, team leaders, and executives.

A right integrated management system will facilitate in promoting collaboration and sharing information. This form of technical integration is important for companies looking to build a corporate community, monitor employee performance, and enhance engagement, if not right away, then in the near future.

How will HR safeguard the company's culture using Technology?

Regardless of the context of your company, there are plenty of HR tech resources, solutions, and channels that can be used to improve your work culture and ensure employee engagement.

There are plenty of AI-enabled or platform-integrated tools that can be used to recognize, perform and reward achievements with reward points, perks, flyer miles, and partnership advantages that enable build the practice of recognition and appreciation.

Using cloud-based Saas solutions to give workers versatility and ability to be flexible and location-agnostic, yet connected, helps create a collaborative culture.

The use of online learning programs and training sessions helps workers keep them regularly updated and upskilled.

A majority of co-working spaces have their integrated co-working management tools that can be great forums to help network, talk about successes, exchange stories and profiles, work together and explore ways to develop your business.

Whether it is a start-up, an SME or a huge organization, creating a healthy corporate culture is not only vital to attracting consumers or for business development, but it is equally important to retain employees' satisfaction as employees are an important clog in the brand's wheel. As the world witnesses shifts in the redistribution of talent, technology, and job redistribution, the co-working community must also learn to go with new trends.

The shift of the work culture⯑

One of the notable revelations in the aftermath of the Covid-19 pandemic is the solid emergence of the 'work-from-home'. The seamless adaptation of a large section of the formal workforce across sectors to work-from-home is a testament to the concept's efficiency and effectiveness.⯑

HR is core at the process of this change; organizations that had invested in HR now enjoy the benefits and stand to benefit during the pandemic when many were caught unaware. Optimal process digitisation and cloud solution adoption enabled companies to make a smooth transition to remote work, ensuring business as usual in an unusual business manner.

Workers embracing the 'work-from-home' model

The skill of collaboration technologies has been a crucial link in facilitating the change and workers have risen to the task in the face of difficulties and adopted the work-from-home practice to make it a success. It is remarkable to see the extent to which workers, armed with the appropriate technologies and tools, can be extraordinarily productive working from home.

So much so, that as we move into a contactless world, there is now a valid point for organizations to make the win-win work-from-home an important component of their HR strategy for the near future. At the core of this transformation will be the Integration of technology and digital tools with people processes.

Virtual Hiring Platforms

In the aftermath of the unexpected devastation of the pandemic, companies are now resorting to cutting-edge virtual hiring solutions as potential candidates can't appear for face-to-face interviews in view of social distancing. As a result, companies face the risk of losing out the top talent workforce. Also, Virtual hiring technologies can prove to be an efficient way of expanding business. Most of the companies are practising the below-mentioned technologies that support the virtual hiring process.

1. LinkedIn Company Page
2. Virtual Careers Fair
3. Scheduled, On Demand, Video Interviewing
4. Live Video Interviewing
5. E-signatures
6. Online Skill and Attainment Testing

How does the technology work?

Virtual platforms enable the talent acquisition team to link with the candidates during the whole video call interview process and can also communicate with the candidates in real-time.

As things stand now, virtual platforms will remain as the mainstay in the post-pandemic environment.

Applying technologies helps in achieving business goals

As the technologies evolved, lots of jobs got automated and the toughest of work got performed for people. Nowadays, technology has reached its peak and even several intellectually complex tasks are being done by machines. It has enabled us to connect with people across any location in the world and anywhere and at any time. This enhanced collaboration provided a high degree of flexibility in communication that makes it easier for working staff, colleagues, and managers to communicate with each other.

Technological wonders

With the use of modern technologies, many jobs have already been fully automated. The integration of three processes – Big Data, IoT, and AI, provides business owners with the data they require to make important decisions. They help in enhancing the efficiency of business practices. ⁇

Big data obtained by LOT sensors help AI to make recommendations based on potential problems or repair work that needs to be done on equipment and as a result, the company owner is fully informed of any technological concerns that will need to be handled in advance. Robots are used in nearly all establishments, where they have displaced most of the staff. They are used to perform roles that employees can't do at home.⁇

YouTube, yet another classic case of technology invention, helps anyone in launching their own YouTube channel and potentially one can acquire stardom status, without the help of Hollywood studio, agents, or networks.

iPhone initiated a handheld technology boom, bringing smartphones to the globe and placing the Internet in everyone's pockets.

Why adaptability becomes the key to success for businesses?

There's no doubt that organizations are rethinking their business models, redesigning work to leverage the potential of technology and adjust to a fast-changing world. Yet for all the technological progress, it's evident they can't thrive without making people a priority.

Technology progress will offer us more efficient means

Evolving technologies will affect the future of work in below-mentioned major categories:

Important Emerging Technologies That Will Recast the Future of Work

The concept of work is evolving fast, and hereunder are the significant emerging technologies affecting the future of work.

Quantum Computing

Quantum computing can support a variety of and virtual reality (VR) and augmented reality (AR) applications. They can make training and diagnostic processes significantly more efficient and accurate.

It can significantly improve cybersecurity, too. This would reduce IT expenditure and enable companies to efficiently safeguard confidential data by leveraging applications of automating tools from cloud storage platforms. It has the ability to derive meaning from vast quantities of data and can be useful in fields as varied as aviation, manufacturing or commerce industry.

Digital Talent Platforms

The skill to tap talent from all over the world through different work arrangements is promoting organizations to review their talent model and employee lifecycle.

Using digital channels decreases the effect of a mismatch between skills, availability, and location. Companies will move from filling specific job "roles" to hiring talent based on the skills needed to complete a project.

Digitally-supported independent workers will be less restricted to a particular job title but have to conform to the priorities of each project to continuously show value.

AI-propelled Technologies

The artificial intelligence (AI) umbrella includes deep learning, machine learning, as well as natural language generation, natural language processing and much more.

The use of AI enables companies to efficiently derive information from their proprietary market data for prompt and reliable decision-making. To generate this business data, organizations, of course, should primarily embrace automation to get this business data.

AI makes work more fun and rewarding by enhancing the competencies of knowledge workers. AI's capacity to process a huge amount of data and retrieve information is critical. It lets people break through the noise to check where they can concentrate efforts on increasing strategic thinking and decision-making.

Visual, Low-code Process Automation

Automation is essential to enhancing efficiency, minimizing human error, and reducing operational costs. Less number of workers will be required for repetitive tasks, and more work staff on strategic decision-making and creative problem-solving.

Automation will encourage businesses that focus on routine procedures to determine whether productivity can be enhanced. They will have to retrain and reallocate staff to take on positions that will leverage the strategic ability to exploit their skills and operational expertise.

Cloud-based Communication Platforms

Unified communications (UC) systems enable companies to take advantage of a remote workforce effectively. Such cloud-based applications enable streamline workflow, promote teamwork and enhance performance.

They facilitate real-time communication and cooperation through features like voice and video calling, instant messaging, as well as screen and file sharing. They enable businesses to get in touch with a global workforce and recruit talent without being impeded by inefficient communications. ⏀

A UC platform that provides a reliable environment for effective communication is the "centre" of a digital workplace. It affects how and where research is performed, triggering a "workplace" rethink and adding a global element to many employees.

Conclusion: In the near future, new automation technologies in areas like Robotics and AI will create some new jobs in the digital technology arena, and through productivity advances, build surplus wealth and spending that will support extra jobs of existing categories. At the same time, employers need to explore ways to make the sure continuance of connectivity and use the right hardware and software to build spaces, locations and employees with each other.⏀

*****

Chapter-4

The Evolution of Leadership

The practice of leadership

Leadership has been a subject of interest since the birth of man, and since the early 20th century, many leadership and management studies were taken up in right earnest. The notable theories that emerged during the 20th century comprise Transformational Theory, Style and Behavioural Theory, Great Man Theory, Process Leadership Theory, Trait Theory, and Transitional and Laissez Fair Leadership Theory.

HR's Influence on the Leadership Development

Developing leadership is important for any company's growth. HR can have a real impact, beyond the basics, in developing the leaders of their company – and not your just present leaders, but also future ones.

One of HR's many responsibilities is to ensure that their company has the best people with the abilities to assume leadership roles and leaders at every level of the organization are successful in given job roles. The more capable your leaders are, the more engaged your workforce becomes, which can result in higher performance and higher value for money.

Here are the five best possible ways in which HR professionals can have a positive effect on the growth of leaders within their organization.

Business Strategy

What are the significant leadership roles that can impact business strategy? Give thought to noting the key responsibilities of leadership roles focused on strategy and recognizing the direct correlation between role and strategy. In this way, you will be able to identify more clearly which leaders have the experience required to take on strategically focused initiatives. ⁇

Current Leaders

Consider look at development areas for existing leaders, and motivate them to enhance their skills. Through celebrating where your present leaders succeed and identifying where they can perform better, you're not only influencing the consistency of the leadership in the company – you are impacting the majority in your workers as well. The stronger your leaders are in inspiring and empowering their employees, the more those employees get engaged and motivated.

Pic: There can be no leaders without followers.

Source: https://www.conselium.com/7-evolving-leadership-qualities-21st-century/

Team Performance

This one builds off of the above level. As leaders motivate their teams; engagement is rising – and so does success. This is where HR plays its role by equipping leaders with resources. Coaching, training, the prospect of working with a mentor, and more – all these steps can be taken by a team member or a staff member. However, the decision rests with HR to implement them. The outcome? A more committed, inspired, successful team of additional workers involved in building their leadership skills – essentially making the investment the company makes in leadership development a future-proofing one.

Rewards Package

Should you not have a bonus program? Consider putting one putting in place, and focusing on leadership. Finding ways to celebrate leadership successes and help staff become more conscious of how the leaders of the organization impact everyone. This can be a huge encouragement for leaders to continue to do what they do and for other workers to feel motivated to accept more job leadership duties. A quick reminder: not all leaders are the kind of social, rally-the-troops, which means that some might be overlooked. Consider blending a rewards program with the company's strategic plan, so that leaders of all kinds get equal importance.

Advocacy

Frequently, team members are going to have a strong idea of who could fit into and excel in specific roles. As an HR professional, inspire your leaders to give a pat to their employees and work with your leaders to best position staff. This will require a thorough understanding of the skills required as a leader and as a worker reporting to the leader – something you maybe knowing a lot about. The objective is to match the right people with the right job, and this is best achieved when HR and organizational leaders combine to build a competent workforce.

How Leadership will change in the coming years?

The ensuing few years will be more about leaders who guide people and then disappear from their way. Unlike routine supervision of tasks, managers and leaders will realize what their employees expect from their job, how to achieve the best possible results for employees, and how to engage and retain them.

Agents of change

In the foreseen period, successful leaders and managers will be those who get out of their comfort zone and embrace – and even drive – change. These leaders have the mettle, strategic focus and insight to take leaps of faith and explore new ways to realize their business objectives. They will support their organization and team's evolution to thrive in a swiftly changing environment.

Ability to find new approaches

Correspondingly, our leaders and administrators of the future will have to be imaginative and innovative as agents of transformation, with a proven capacity to come up with new ideas. Shifting business landscapes and disruptive technology means seizing new opportunities with fresh ideas. Such leaders, rather than being passive and reactive, would succeed in influencing the effect of the disruptive forces of change.

Leading the Economy of Wisdom

When companies make a transition from traditional workplace models of top-down, siloed, and hierarchical structures, leaders and managers need to embrace cultures and teams that represent the economy based on experience, not expertise. Knowledge and information are omnipresent, so to stay competitive you require doing more with what you are aware of. Supporting diversity of thought, along with continuous evolution, holds the key.

Create new growth areas

In the coming years, the best leaders and administrators will effectively steer their company and employees through the major cultural demographic change already underway. These leaders will identify it as an opportunity for growth and take advantage of tactics such as cultural fluidity and intelligence, modern team building and new marketing strategies replicating the new cultural demographics. Such leaders should diversity as not a cost centre, but a new profit centre for strategic development, encompassing both talent and business.

Quickly identify and close opportunities gaps

Tomorrow's successful leaders and managers are the ones who can recognize and close opportunities gaps in their market. In doing so, competitive threats will be effectively managed as they rise and anticipate developments and solutions. Widening observations to identify opportunities, discovering new frontiers and identifying timing and depth of opportunities are important elements of this trait.

Such leaders will be creative in addressing opportunities gaps and will find new ways to do things and push their team to grow towards achieving goals.

Outcome Monitoring only

The top managers of the future may be those who concentrate solely on the results, rather than the work of team members as to how and where. The most efficient managers will act to build work environments where the focus is on production and performance, rather than logged hours and processes. It represents an increasingly autonomous and independent workforce and the effect could be increasing job satisfaction and employee enablement. Leaders will require excellent communication skills and the capacity to maintain relationships.

Fascinating communicators

The future leaders and managers maybe those who communicate well in a personalized yet contextualized way. Such visionary leaders inspire workers and accelerate transformation by sharing personal stories and concrete examples, as well as basing their narrative in the sense of organization. Such leaders may use the method of personal contact to build an inclusive team atmosphere and display concern for progress and well-being.

A positive narrative will result in a quicker transition, faster team members buy-in, and a cohesive team or organizational culture that promotes the growth of the organization.

Self-discovery

Leaders and administrators of 2020 and beyond will be ready for self-discovery. They will be interested to explore biases and how they affect their own decision-making process. These members will remain open to diverse views while being open to self-discovery. They will be successful in managing diversity this way and will be skilled in encouraging and building on employee input. This can result in more cohesive teams, better worker satisfaction, higher productivity and improved organizational performance.

Managing soft-skills

By 2020, leaders and executives should be specialists by determining candidates' social skills, as well as their technical abilities. Team members will not only need to be analytically competent; they need soft skills such as creative problem-solving skills and people skills. Managers who can recognize and handle these competencies would be well-positioned to build effective teams.

Comfortable in dealing with the unknown

In the coming years, the top leaders and executives will be at ease in dealing with turmoil, uncertainty, and the unknown. They will succeed and work well when things are not explicitly defined or predictable, and they must remain fast and agile in order to adapt to a changing operating environment quickly and effectively. It will be these leaders who are ideally positioned to push their teams and companies to the next level.

Emotional Intelligence

When we leave behind the top-down systems and march towards flatter and less hierarchical organizations, leaders and managers require being emotionally savvy individuals who can realize and invest in their people to motivate them to prosper. Traits such as responsibility, openness, justice, integrity and capacity to build systems and processes for humans may not be replaceable in the near future by AI tools. As such, they will be invaluable in the future leaders of the coming years.

Conclusion: Leadership is the capacity to lead a group of individuals to realize a collective purpose. It is achieved by individuals adding their qualities to leadership. Successful organizations can't let leaders run with old-fashioned leadership practises or in a silo. The current generation's leaders require to continually enhance their skills to successfully collaborate and meet the growing needs of today's knowledge worker. ⏹

*****

Chapter 5

Preparing your organization for new employment methods

An overview of Talent Management Strategies

Companies are as strong as their employees, which is why having talent management right is important for today's competitive climate. From identifying and recruiting to hiring and cultivating talent, companies need to ensure that their talent management tactics help their overall strategic planning and company goals. Identifying and recruiting the best possible people who can fit within an organization's culture and contributing to it can be quite big challenges and an opportunity.

Often, HR professionals face issues related to employee relations in the workplace and are clueless about deciding the best approach to coping with these issues. This is where the need arises for setting standards for developing the companies' policies. Working out such a strategy enables a company as to how to manage organizational circumstances consistently. ⏎

Strategies for talent management should lead to a high-performing workforce, a system that identifies and enhances weak areas, and the means for drawing, developing, and retaining quality, varied talent.

Employment practises when hiring workers

The below-mentioned recruiting approaches will serve well an organization when recruiting employees:

Inclusive Job Announcements:

The terms you use, the format of the document, as well as the way you say things will put off the entire candidate population groups (women, ethnic minorities, and the elderly). Job offers should be short. Ads written succinctly are generally filled quicker and attract the attention of more applications. Stating the values and purpose of the company will help the candidates decide it is an environment where they want to work in.

Video Interview:

This one is very self-explanatory. At the same time, it is not a less effective method of recruitment. Quite the contrary, when you have candidates living abroad, using video technology can be a great option; it saves both yourself and your candidate a lot of time – and money – and you can still benefit from a much larger pool of applicants.

Programmatic Advertising:

Can we call programmatic advertising still an innovative method of recruitment? Perhaps not, but it's something you can certainly consider when hiring online.

Programmatic advertising refers to the automatic posting of work advertising that targets the work profiles you're searching for.

Nonetheless, hiring on niche platforms where the target candidates are hanging out can be relatively creative. Except when Amazon publishes Tinder work adverts, or when Goldman Sachs uses Spotify.

Here the key takeaway is: Know your candidates. And if you do so, you can use programmatic ads – or any form of recruiting – to make sure your work advertisement.

Take advantage of the gig economy

It is an increasingly successful recruiting technique. Often you need someone who has different expertise – let's say a graphic designer – and you need them as soon as possible. But in fact, you require them just for a couple of high-priority projects that need to be completed on short notice.

Hiring a freelancer to get the job done is a wise thing to do

Just rely on one of the different platforms out there and recruit a freelancer. Since you don't have to go through the normal recruiting process, it will save you a lot of time and money.

Working with freelancers also gives you the chance to see how successful they are, and how will they are interacting with the rest of the work team. When you like what you see, you know whom you're looking for a full- time employee to recruit next time!⏾

Passive candidates

Inactive candidates have long been a bit of a concealed treasure. It was almost difficult to establish contacts with these skilled staff in the pre-social media era, who are not trying to shift jobs.

The advent of professional social networks has been a real game-changer.

Recruiters can now reach out to anyone – including inactive candidates. They can engage and build a relationship with those candidates.

Employee referrals

As regards recruitment methods, employee referrals are among the most successful recruitment methods. The new hires referred to tend to be more engaged, more productive and less likely to quit.

To build your own employee referral program you must ensure that it contains the following elements:

➢ Incentives: Usually, cash incentives are highly effective. At the same time, non-monetary rewards such as extra vacations or special gifts can do the trick, too.

➢ Ease of use: Keep the referral program as user-friendly as possible. No lengthy forms to fill in, keep it short and simple, or heaps of papers.

Pic: The Winning way of Recruiting Culture and Talent Fit

Source: resources.workable.com

Texting

Admittedly, texting may not be very creative itself. However, it can be super successful as a recruiting tool. Nearly 98% of sent text messages are being read. Also, the text response rate is 45% (as opposed to just 6% for emails).

As such, texting is a smart way to:

➢ Check-in with candidates.

➢ Schedule appraisals and interviews.

➢ Get in touch with applicants during the recruitment process.

In the world of social media, the importance of social media is growing all the time. If you haven't initiated using social media as a part of your online recruitment activities, it's time to get going. Especially, younger generations of job aspirants rely on social channels when looking for a job (86% to be precise).

Virtual Reality

Increasingly, a large number of companies are using different virtual reality experiences to show candidates that they are a thrilling and innovative work atmosphere to work.

What kind of experience does that look like?

For instance, VR can give your (remote) candidates a practical, virtual tour or the workplace, or show your corporate culture to the applicants. The VR headsets have a higher level of realism and clarity compared with a video. Not necessarily, it has to be all that expensive either!

Dealing with the Aging workforce

This may not be the first that comes to my mind when you think of creative forms of recruitment. Yet, the global population is ageing rapidly; 10,000 people turn 65 every day in the US.

You see, the reality is there are more skilled, experienced people than young people all over the world. Even if you boast of the best recruitment strategy in the world, there is a paucity of young working talent.

Fostering creativity among employees

Although innovation can be a great resource for business leaders searching for creative approaches to current problems, spreading in any workplace can be a challenging job. Companies setting eyes on growth must tap into innovative energies. It is going to become essential to drive the business forward.

With a clear perception of the strategies that inspire creativity and innovation, managers may promote growth among employees and teams.

Making the workplace a breeding ground for creativity has many advantages and can result in great success. The below tips should be considered by companies hoping to inspire innovation among employees:

- **Motivate Teamwork and Individualism**: The odd thing about cooperation is that both individuality and selfishness are required to proceed. It is vital that managers not only encourage team building and collective work but also make sure that employees do not check their individuality at the door. Many creative ideas come not from just one person but are shaped to become fully formed by a team.

- **Don't be shy of being open to feedback**: The brainstorming process can be delicate and complex, especially when a large team is involved in finding an acceptable solution. In these environments, making fast decisions about an idea is simple, and dismissing it as inappropriate. Instead of stymying growth by allowing negativity, encourage constructive and additive feedback.

- **Expand your team:** One simple and quick way to promote creativity at the workplace is to add different perspectives, insights, and learning styles. Diverse teams are more likely to result in exchanging of creative ideas when people are pressed for a solution in different ways.

Being creative helps workers too

Creativity will emerge as the third most important skill factor for employees by 2020, next to complex problem-solving and critical thinking. Possessing more creative skills helps employees feel confident and innovative. People require new skills and the capability to learn and adapt to these conditions on a continuous basis. To have a successful future career, workers need to have fresh ideas, the ability to overcome difficult challenges and think outside the box.

Conclusion: Recruitment has never been so challenging and exciting! - Just as it is today. When you desire to get the best applicants you need to be imaginative and every now and then seek some new, inventive recruiting methods. Employers should ensure that they're building a viable community and working on it day by day.

Doing so sends signals to prospective candidates that you're an exciting business environment to work with, you embrace technology, and you put great emphasis on the candidate experience.

*****

Chapter 6

The four C's that will thrive in the Future Workplace

The fundamentals of an individual's success

Today's life is more complex than it was a half-century ago. With a host of problems coupled with instant access to a global society, civil literacy in our schools could not be more important. The world is confronted by a host of problems such as global warming, pandemic diseases, immigration reforms, and financial meltdowns. Students and working professionals need to develop a strong understanding of issues and need to have certain basic skills to interact, cooperate, think critically and create.

Pitfalls in the communication system

The present education system is not tuned to respond to an evolving world and what was considered a good education 50 years ago is no longer enough in the 21st century for success in college, career and citizenship. They must introduce practical techniques for integrating the 'Four C's' into the classroom atmosphere and work atmosphere setting; tools for developing better technology skills; and methods for ensuring students and working staff learn in a meaningful context.

The Significance of 4 C's at the workplace

We live in a world that requires people who can communicate, solve problems, work together, and be creative. As our global economy expands, it becomes even more imperative that we build this next generation for new careers.

Employers look for the people who are adaptable, flexible to acquire new skills, and who have a reasonable interpersonal skill level. This is where the four C's fit into the requirements of employers.

In today's digital world, career success means uninterrupted evolution and learning, adapting your technical competencies and the most basic features of learning and thinking.

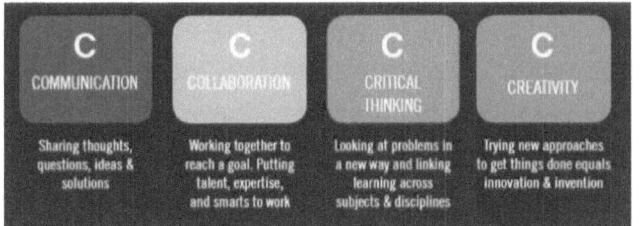

Pic Title: The Defined Framework for the Future of Work⬚

Source: edureach101.com

Four Professional Competencies - Essential to succeed in the 21ˢᵗ century

To get noticed by employers, employees need to be well-versed with 4 important qualities known as the C's: Creativity, Communication, Collaboration, and Critical Thinking.

Being aware of applying these four ideas will enable employees to prepare them to adapt and prosper in their careers, today and in our unreliable future.

1. **Creativity:** Creative is often compared to the creative arts or literature. Once you have recognized the best issues to solve, it often requires creativity to solve them. To be creative at work, not necessarily you need to be in a creative field. Creativity in every field ultimately means taking ideas and turning them into

reality. More specifically, it's about exploring ways to get more meaningful results (quicker, cheaper, superior value for clients), by carrying out a task or finishing a project differently than before. Innovative ideas need not be big and mind-blowing. More often than not, it is the workers who find ways to improve a job. As workers we tend to think if we have an idea, it would not be appreciated or if it was a good suggestion, someone else would have suggested.

2. **Collaboration:** Today, collaboration is at the heart of the most successful businesses in the world. As competition intensifies, it is imperative to foster creativity among employees through teamwork. Whenever employees work together, their ability to learn and grow extends beyond their comfort zones and takes businesses to new heights. Also, it enables individuals to increase their productivity and encourage healthy relationships among employees. Workers benefit from learning each other through collaboration.

There are several other reasons for motivating collaboration. For example, working in close operation with colleagues, challenges people to think properly and express their ideas clearly. This also helps them to get clarification on their key competencies. Thus, workers get a greater understanding of their strengths and limitations. It helps them to work together more efficiently by plugging the skill gaps of each other. Further, collaboration enables workers to be more accountable and empowered, particularly when teams are remotely at work.

3. **Critical thinking:** In every century, critical thinking has remained unchanged in every century and profession. To be competitive in the 21st century, you have to understand the reality, no matter how high technology the machine is; it's worthless without a human instructing it what to do and thinking critically about the outcome. Vitally, it has a due role to play at the workplace and the employer's value workers who are critically aware of how to think. Critical thinkers bring creative solutions to the table and helping companies innovate to stay competitive. ⍰

Developing critical thinking competencies will make an individual a better candidate for the new position or promotion. Employees would have to come up with ideas that are absolutely unique.

4. **Communication**: Communication revolves around exchanging thoughts, questions, proposals and solutions. In the technology era, it is much easier and at the same time difficult to communicate. At the same, this could be the easiest of the four to practice. Technology has brought us more convenient ways to communicate.

By functioning as part of a team, employees can complete their tasks quicker and more effectively than those who work alone. Employers on their part need to create a technology-friendly atmosphere at the workplace wherein employees can learn appropriate ways of communication through technology.

HR's initiatives on the Future of Work

The future of work calls for the HR to invest in building a community in which creativity flourishes, collaboration is promoted, and communication is inspired. Collaboration not only denotes the cooperation between teams and functions but also between HR heads and employees.

Managing organizational communication

Critical thinking is one of the most important qualities in HR for anyone. Whether you work in a recruitment role, a benefit and a payroll role, or more in a generalist job role, you certainly have to deal with your communication style, but the communication style of your peers, subordinates and senior management.

It's important that HR works to ensure coordination through the company, because without consistent communication, the offer letter may be prepared incorrectly. Benefits that are not described correctly can result in workers with negative attitudes. Also, when you hire a new worker, negotiate pay enhances, or decide how to deal with employee grievances, it is imperative that you analyse the situation and make decisions critically.

Handling tough situations with critical thinking abilities

Critical thinking enables HR professionals to cope with a tough situation with ease. Either it is dispute management or solving issues with employees, critical thinking helps the HR to rebuild or bring out opinions and proposals that work better with the work environment.

HR can help create collaboration among employees

Companies are now recruiting the best-talented workforce from all over the country. It is important that the HR department provides a collaborative work atmosphere for both staff and candidates. From day one, it should be easy to talk to recruiters, hiring managers, and those who influence hiring decisions.

As Collins and Smith observed, HR plays a vital role in inspiring and empowering people to work together. To connect individual behaviour with corporate results, many high-tech companies are now offering employees at all levels – the company's stock or stock options.

By collaborating with Microsoft Teams, HR can invite someone to join Microsoft Teams for chatting individually or within a group that has candidates and decision-makers in an organization. Using Skype, the HR can facilitate the business voice conversation or video conversation call for the workforce in seconds.

HR' role in fostering creativity within the workforce

Creativity and innovative are inborn in every employee. Yet, many companies are stopping it from thriving - unknowingly. Many companies fall short when it comes to promoting creativity and innovation in their workforce.

As such when searching for innovation, HR needs to ask specific questions and learn from people how innovation presents itself in them as we all have it. HR, therefore, has a role to play if it wishes businesses to fall into the creative and living pool of companies rather than stagnant and dying. If you want to nurture innovation and creativity in individuals, you will have to make available training materials and enable employees, for instance, to have a growth mindset, resilience, and grit.

Beyond the recruitment stage, the next step for HR is to provide employees with the right tools and framing works to hone and develop their creative skills.

HR's challenges in implementing the business model for companies

The real challenge is – what are you doing to positively impact your staff's attitude towards being supportive with customers, performing at a high level and contributing to your organization?

The key is to understand how your workers prefer to work. The HR can then develop the management of change plan and digital workforce strategy that aligns with your needs organizations function in the community.

Conclusion: All four of the identified C's are essential skills for people to grow and they are creating learning experiences for us as educators. To master the four "Cs", employees of the 21st-century employees require tapping technology to be successful problem-solvers, collaborators, communicators and creators.

*****

Chapter 7

Virtual Training is here to stay: Are you ready to implement it?

How does 'Training' add value to a company?

Companies who have invested in teaching and learning culture have always had better retention levels of their staff because workers feel their organization is genuinely safeguarding their professional development and making a direct investment in them.

The strategic role of Learning and Development

In the last decade, many training delivery methods have developed with advancements in technology. Organizations are increasingly relying on learning and development (L&D) to complement their business strategy by drawing, developing and retaining top talent. Apart from the type of training to be provided, the method of training itself is a critical aspect to consider.

When the corporate training market bursts with training delivery methods, the best strategy for L&D practitioners is not the new training delivery method, but the right training delivery method to suit their needs.

Choosing a training delivery method

Choosing a training method may be a tough task, given the number of factors, including the budget, size and type of staff, location, timetable, and objectives. L&D practitioners also assess implementation strategies based on the overall learning objectives of the company. A majority of them employ multiple delivery methods because a single modality can't do everything well.

The following are some of the top choices and you can select the methods of providing training that match your organizational needs.

1. **Instructor-led Training:** Instructor-led training, or classroom training, is the most traditional method of training that is best suited for creating an overall understanding of the subject of training. As per the observation of the Training Industry, Inc. Research, ILT is the most favoured training method for learners, with 55

% of learners expressing their preference for this method.

ILT can be effective in delivering a comparatively limited amount of knowledge to a wide number of learners in a short time, with the only added benefit being the instructor's reputation and his teaching skills. The important benefit of ILT is the obvious interactivity, as learners can ask questions and obtain immediate answers.

2. **Virtual Classrooms:** Although ILT continues to be prevalent, technological advances have led to the use of or virtual instructor-led training (VILT) or virtual classrooms. Digital classrooms allow organizations to offer text, video and documents in real-time. ⍰

   They can provide training from anywhere, and learners are at advantage of attending sessions from wherever they are located. This saves organizations valuable time and money on logistics and locations. Good virtual trainers still have a human touch.

   VILT is most effective when organizations are required to train a large group but there is no dedicated venue, or the learners (and instructors) are dispersed geographically. It's also successful only when the organization musters good tech support for the trainers and the learners.

3. **E-learning:** E-learning is one of the widely popular forms of training delivery available today. Research indicates that global e-learning is expected to reach over $300 billion in size by 2025, and e-learning is used by 77% of US-based organizations. Such online learning services use a combination of audio and video text; discussion forums; and/or interactive assessment.

E-learning is a good alternative for organizations looking to provide flexible learning opportunities in less period time to a global audience by delivering collaborative and engaging training programs in the form of videos, games, HTML, quizzes and other forms of content. E-learning is also appropriate for organizations that need to provide a learning environment for high-risk learners to perform tasks.

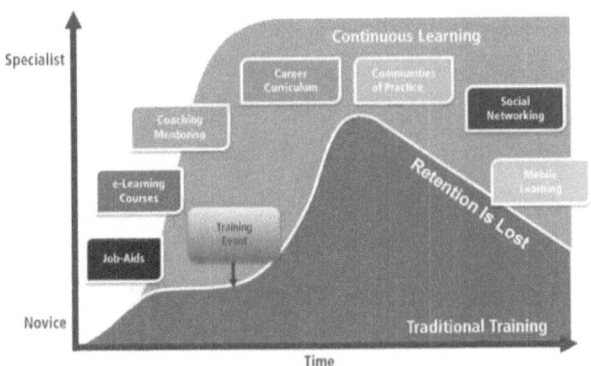

Pic: Creating a learning culture is a must to get a competitive advantage.

4. **Mobile learning:** Although mobile learning is a relatively new training delivery method, it is increasingly provided by prominent organizations as it offers the host of benefits, such as the ability to deliver training anytime, any location and on any device and in the form micro-learning, social learning, short how-to videos and other engaging formats.

    Mobile learning is also popular in offices, although it is best suited to the needs of on-the-go or on-the-go workers. In certain situations, the nature of the business (for instance, oil and mining) requires operating in areas with little Internet access, rendering an offline smartphone learning device or platform the go-to solution.

5. **Blended learning:** With blended learning, organizations can leverage a combination of approaches to ensure that each learner retains information. A combined learning method is suitable for organizations with specific curriculum criteria and dynamic learning goals.

   Among all the training delivery methods, blended learning will be ideal for organizations with different training needs and complex learning goals.

The HR's role in making Effective Corporate e-Learning Culture

There is no doubt that online training and courses have provided ample opportunities for personal and professional development in the corporate world; particularly in the field of human resources. Continuing online training is important to the bottom-line of the company's well-being.

A supportive and strong corporate e-Learning Culture is the foundation of a company's e-Learning strategy. It makes sure that you maintain company-wide standards that make your employees accountable.

Here're the seven qualities of an effective corporate e-Learning culture that every HR of the organization should aim for:

1. **Open Communication:** Employees must get the satisfaction that they have the freedom to express their thoughts and suggestions without the fear of being punished. Also, on-line instructors and facilitators need to be ready to give quick feedback to enhance performance.

   An effective corporate e-Learning culture depends on open and transparent communication. All parties concerned require working with each other to overcome hurdles. Often, this goes hand in hand with openness and mutual respect.

   Employees enter the workplace with precognitions. These beliefs, views, and values have a direct effect on which they are as individuals. Therefore, any member of your staff will appreciate and value the expertise of others. The outcome is an uncomfortable workplace where employees have apprehensions to voice their concerns.

2. **Support:** Even the most seasoned team member requires guidance with their online preparation from time to time. If they obtain

that help, they will push past boundaries to broaden their skills.

On the other side, not getting the support they need will stifle their career growth. Even if workers may not need it, the will still have connections to online help services. These can be achieved in the context of email addresses, FAQs, web guides, and peer-based communities.

You can also offer one-on-one support to the employees with an online mentorship training program.

3. **Employee Focus:** Training objectives are important, however, they don't serve any purpose if your employees are not braced up for the challenge.

This is why a large number of Fortune 500 companies are now incorporating wellness programs into their online training strategies. Meditation, Yoga and other relaxation exercises enable workers to move back from online training and reflect on their wellbeing.

Rather than designing lengthy online courses that provide a variety of information, online training becomes more specific digestible. Incorporate regular gaps into the training style, as well as spaced e-Learning tasks so that staff set pace themselves. Employee-centric and results-driven professional educational systems are identical.

4. **Strong Leadership:** Every manager, supervisor, and senior executive should be in your corner. Such people are the ones that lead by example, and the workers look to them for direction.

   They need to aware of how to make the best use of the online training platform and suggest the right online resources based on the requirements of staff.

   For instance, workers who fail to complete the given task should be provided with additional support and online training tools. Eventually, your leadership team is largely accountable for enhancing efficiency at the departmental level. As such, they should get all the online learning they need, such as lessons and demos, before beginning an online training course.

5. **Personal Accountability:** Employees will be made responsible for their acts and behaviour. More specifically, there will be repercussions if the requirements are not complied with. In some cases, training contracts can remedy this

problem by offering each staff member an individualized online training plan.

However, working staff should also feel professionally accountable and invest time in academic preparation (online training). When they realize that there is a scope for change, they ought to identify that and decide whether to plug the holes. Denial is the enemy of prosperity and personal development.

6. **Self-empowered:** Quite frequently, employees feel that online training is above their control. They are clueless about what they do, what they're working for, or whether they're utilizing online services.

A positive organizational culture in e-Learning relies on self-empowerment and self-confidence. Employees deserve to realize that their opinions and feelings do count, no matter where they are on the organizational ladder. Everyone is a valued member of your e-Learning team, and they need to be reminded of that now and then.

Don't hesitate to praise when the appreciation is earned. Provide them with direct reviews so that they can recognize their abilities. You may also suggest leader boards and other gamification mechanisms that develop their self-confidence.

7. **Goal-centric:** Effective corporate culture e-Learning revolves around goals and priorities. Every online training course, operation and support aligns with the preferred outcome. This requires a well-crafted objective statement, online training instructions, as well as clear expectations.

Larger goals can be split into smaller targets to let online training more manageable. Therefore, organizations will review their online workplace training policy regularly to recognize opportunities for change.

Further, they will initiate steps anytime when a problem occurs and utilize all available online resources to strengthen their strategy. In addition to this, every member of the team must be granted the ability to accomplish their own goals. It involves the availability of just-in-time online training tools and personalized online training paths.

Promoting a positive organizational e-Learning community needs more than just preparation. Organizations need to be proactive on this and set an example. Your online training program requires to be promoted by managers, supervisors and executives. They have to convince your staff that their commitment, energy, and devotion are going to be rewarded in spades. Otherwise, you can notice that inspiration, or lack of motivation, is becoming the main problem.

HR should strive to build a learning culture among employees

Building a learning atmosphere is a continuous task for HR. While ensuring that it meets present and potential future business needs, HR needs to identify the potential of teams or people who require developing their competencies and strengths.

Giving workers information on the potential abilities they may need and encouraging them to take control of their learning is deemed critical to developing a culture of learning.

How can HR focus on changing its training style for the future of work?⯑

The most critical part to bear in mind is to ensure that your programs add value to the company. Training and Learning & Development programs should be unique to the company they serve. HR needs to ensure that the Learning and Development Programs sync with the goals of the organization.

Below are a few suggestions about how organizations should help their workers make the best out of every training and learning opportunity.

1. Assign people roles/assignments: Empower employees to make choices.
2. Cross-train workers: Promote it from inside.
3. Let employees understand that you are investing in their future development: Take appropriate steps to arrange required training and optional training for varied disciplines. Inspire employees to follow their curiosity.
4. Implement technology that workers already want to use: For instance, training workers on social networking sites in which they are already active (Facebook or Slack for the Q&A Forum, YouTube for training videos).
5. Ensure managers are a part of training programs: Ask them to share responsibilities with employees for drawing up individual development plans for their direct reports.

6. Expose your staff to independent thinking: If it's through visiting professional network sites such as Udemy, inviting industry luminaries to the organization for fireside chats or putting aside a fund for workers to join business conferences, employees may acquire experience and develop innovative thinking out of exposure to conversing with outsiders.

7. Tap into your work staff to unearth hidden talents: Call them to help each other.

8. Adapt training methods to suit the requirements of today's workforce: It's time for businesses to wake up and embrace new, insightful and interactive preparation approaches that address the requirements of today's workforce.

9. Cultivate technology training program for the benefit of employees: Adapt training programs to suit individual learning styles. Also, it is important to have everyone on board while planning for the new technology strategy.

Challenges for HR while implementing the learning culture

HR will have to face many challenges such as identifying and analysing emerging jobs, declining skills, and adding new skills. To tackle this, HR needs to put in place a yearly process to establish a short, mid- as well as long-term competence strategy.

Conclusion: In the coming years, technology will make learning much easier than now and much more of it will occur outside of school environments, both will reduce the value of classrooms and teachers as we know them today. Online courses will get a big lift from advancements in virtual reality (VR), augmented reality (AR), and artificial intelligence (AI).

*****

Chapter 8

The Re-working of work-skills for future jobs

Future of work

There is no doubt that the future of work is transforming. The world continues to evolve through changes in globalization, economics, infrastructure and policy. No matter what field you're in, the capabilities and innovations required to thrive are continually changing – more than ever.

Due to an increase in Automation, AI, and other technologies, the half-life skills of skills have dropped to about five years.

These disruptive forces compel organizations to change rapidly – and they require their people to agile and adaptable to that change.

If you continue to have an eye on the willingness of recruits to acquire new skills, you may begin to build a population where reskilling in an agile fashion can at least be a possibility. Otherwise, you will have to focus on external expertise checks, which is a tough ride in a complex labour market.

The criticality of Reskilling

It's a continuous journey of learning, particularly in today's dynamic workplace, where there is nothing addressed as job security but only employee assessment creation. Technology is constantly witnessing a change and new business models are being developed and heightened customer expectations. Effectively, it means, if you are unable to cope with changing times, you are unemployed. There is, therefore, an urgent need for reskilling to survive in a constantly evolving corporate world.

Recognizing and Marketing Reskilling opportunities in your current employees

The out-dated method of thinking about labour problems needs to be replaced with something new and ideally tailored to the situation. For instance, let's presume an organization has prompted us to use chatbots to take charge of a variety of regular customer service functions. In the old way of looking at it, that sort of automation will inevitably contribute to a contraction in the customer care staff through layoffs.⁇

But a different way of thinking would suggest that your company is going to be the best served by reskilling/upskilling these workers so that they can afford to work with the organization. Many workers who have the ability to withstand the pressure of layoffs will be all the more loyal to your organization. ⁇

Training and recruitment activities should give preference to applicants who have shown the potential to easily develop new skills. Yet, you should take a glance at the present workforce and find workers who are ideal for reskilling opportunities.

The aim should be to identify employees who have been with the firm for at least five years (since they are aware of the corporate culture and general business) and who still possess "adjacent abilities" similar to what you're trying to build and employ. Obviously, they may be interested in reskilling themselves to stay viable and relevant to the organization and advance their career growth. Evidence has shown, after all, that a large number of individuals identify the absence of on-going training and education as a justification for quitting their jobs. Strong reskilling programs will help both retention and recruitment, thereby potentially saving the company's money.

Identifying workers for reskilling programs relies on first understanding what capabilities are available at the workplace. Conducting certain kinds of product skills will serve as a starting point for figuring out who possess adjacent skills that are similar to you know or may use in the immediate future. ⁇

Another part of this is how you should set up some reskilling programs. This needs to be achieved strategically to make things as appealing as possible, which ensures that you have to approach it in part from the point of view of "what's in it for me" for every employee. Work with your marketing team to create a message that can help you "offer" reskilling programs.

Building Reskilling/Up skilling-Ready Workers by Recruiting

Tackling skill gaps in any organization can be done with a two-pronged strategy. The first approach is to put in place strong in-house reskilling/upskilling programs to recognize and retain existing workers to the extent possible. The second approach is to build a workforce that is prepared for reskilling by ensuring that anyone you recruit will acquire new things easily.

You can, of course, inquire about their past history in learning and the introduction of new skills. However, you have to maximize efforts to reach this level. You must carefully evaluate the soft skills and personalities of candidates to learn new skills and deal with unpredictable situations by quickly learning new information.⏎

Some companies utilize games, augmented reality, and entertainment during the recruitment process to learn how to cope with emerging problems and problem-solving through accelerated learning. You want people who are smart, excel in troubleshooting, who knows how to solve issues through technology and who could learn quickly.

The growth of the digital economy scares to leave behind a growing number of employees who may be short of technical expertise needed to respond to the fast change of space in what skills organizations need to push on. Smart staffs see the writing on the wall and take their steps to build the skills that can make them relevant.

Smart organizations ensure that their staffs are made up of workers who are prepared for reskilling and upskilling and create the appropriate learning and training systems required to improve and reskilling of workers if needed. ⁣

When you find like a business is of this curve, you're not alone. They're crucial to continuing to fix the company's condition right now. The accelerated speed of transition and the ever-shorter half-life of abilities do not unexpectedly alter their course. The speed of the transition can only get quicker, so the half-life of ability can only get shorter. There can't a better time than now to act!⁣⁣

The Need for Constant Reskilling: It's time for HR to get involved

There is a real opportunity for HR to take the lead in calling for continuous skills, lifelong employability, whatever we want to address it.

HR needs to consider the following factors in its future skill journey:

<u>Communicate:</u> The HR is constantly required to connect with employees on the need to learn and re-learn. Although companies provide workers with a range of learning tools, it is essential that

employees still recognize the necessity for continuous learning.

Introduce new modes of learning: The HR should experiment with learning modes such as gamified-based learning and e-learning models like microlearning, learning apps. This is an interesting and ever-changing space. ⍰

Create a learning culture: Any investment made by a company does not succeed in the long term until there is a conducive learning culture that not just promotes but still embraces learning.

The Performance Management System and Rewards and Recognition Framework should make it easier for workers to build their skills. Refreshments and mistakes during the period of learning should not be contemplated against the workers. Around the same time, leadership will foster a learning culture to support skill investment.

Concentrate on workforce planning and talent assessment: Through an all-inclusive approach to the workforce, HR can plan what skills it requires to buy, develop or borrow. This, combined with the mid-and long-term needs assessment, will enable companies to recognize skilling, reskilling and upskilling decisions.

Pic: Reskilling – The Only Way Forward for Developing Competencies for future jobs

Source: Shutterstock.com

The World Economic Forum's Findings on a Reskilling Revolution

According to the recent report released by the World Economic Forum on a Reskilling Transition, 95% of the 1.4 million American workers predicted to be displaced from their positions over the next decade will be re-skilled into new employment with higher employment remuneration at a cost of $34 billion.

The same report noted that the private sector could rehabilitate 25% of all at-risk employees with a positive cost-benefit balance for an overall investment of $4.7 billion. The World Economic Forum suggested companies to identify the five quickest-growing jobs and commit to recruiting equal working numbers of men and women.

Source: Weforum.org

How Reskilling and Upskilling are important to every generation of the workforce?

Rather than continuously recruiting and firing, companies have begun to invest in retraining and reskilling to tackle the skills shortage and to overcome management issues. Despite technologies advancing at such an accelerated pace, tomorrow's workforce would need to be educated and established in-house by a mix of preparation, opportunities and community.

Benefits of Reskilling

Profitability is a big problem for companies, but there are also other advantages of reskilling and up skillings, such as physical and mental wellbeing, taxation and reduced welfare costs.

As such, it is always in the government's benefit to engage in reskilling workers. Regular learning and development solutions are cost-effective when compared to hiring additional workers.

The task of reskilling and upskilling is specific for each sector and market, but there is a range of guidelines that are the key to progress in each company.⸮

Reskilling considerations for companies

Don't Recruit on the Ability Alone:

Instead of concentrating on particular abilities and technical knowledge, find someone who is educated and has the zeal to learn. Acquiring new skills can be done quickly for somebody with an adjacent skill set.

Ahead of posting a job opening, search internally for someone who is ready and able to transition to a new role through retraining. Soft skills, expertise, and enthusiasm are becoming highly relevant in the workforce.

Establish Unique Training Programs:

Through MOOCs and other training courses, boot camps and academic lectures, there is a range of options to develop your employees with more up-to-date expertise. By committing to a lifestyle of constant learning, this will contribute to rapid development, greater productivity and higher-paying, happier workers.

With the accessibility of so many learning opportunities, it is important to work with seasoned practitioners who are knowledgeable in your industry practices. Resourcing Edge can help you recognize and address your organization's unique needs.

Conclusion: HR has a chance to shape the future of the workplace and help companies and working staff in this age of transformation. It will also help HR pitch the case for investing in reskilling programs. At the same time, this will create an environment in which employees can thrive, and feel supported in their career goals rather than afraid of losing their jobs.

At the same time, there is an urgent need for senior executives of large companies to reconsider and reshape their role in enabling workers to build the right skills for a rapidly changing economy. The typical person joining the workforce in 2030 would have to prepare and upgrade his or her abilities 8 to 10 times throughout their life.

*****

Chapter 9

What the next 20 years will mean for jobs?

An overview

As the world around us changes dynamically and rapidly, the jobs of the next decade will look quite different from the jobs of the past. Though technology has been a big disruptor to many of the most common jobs in the world, the technology industry has not picked up its pace when compared to other important industries. The next two decades will witness a full-scale revolution in our working lives.

The healthcare industry is expected to see a surge in the coming decade. In reality, the top three fast-paced industries – hospitals, home healthcare and financial insurance – all come under its category.

Cognizant's assessment on the future job scenario

The Cognizant Technology Solution's Centre for the Future of Work (CFW) Research predicts that almost 21 million jobs will be generated in the next 10 to 15 years, causing a surge of mass hiring.

According to the World Economic Forum's Report on the Future of Employment, about 5 million workers will be lost in 15 big developing and growing economies by 2020. Nonetheless, several occupations based on consistency, predictability and routine would be out of reach. Several new careers that require creative problem-solving scenarios, strategic thought and innovation will be on the rise.

Source: https://www.cognizant.com/futureofwork/

The World Economic Forum predicts 5 major changes in the foreseeable future:

- AI together with Robotics will eventually create more employment. Much like today.

- There won't be a lack of jobs however if we fail to take correct steps – lack of skilled talent to recruit those jobs.

- Technological change will keep rising. As such acquiring new skills will be a necessity throughout life.

- The large part of the workforce will become freelance by 2027.

- As remote work becomes reality. Uninterrupted on-site work will give people new geographical freedom to reside where they desire. Cities and metropolitan regions will vie for attracting this new mobile workforce.

Five key forces that are going to determine the future jobs are:

1. Adapt to swift technological change

The world of work is being reshaped by artificial intelligence (AI), the Internet of Things, Robots, and autonomous vehicles. Today's environment needs a workforce that can cope with uncertainty, adapt to regular changes, engage with automation and develop knowledge when certain skills become obsolete.

Deloitte presages that smart professionals and market executives will be searching for ways to generate market value and competitive advantage through technological advances.

A large part of the future of jobs will revolve around Robots

Source: forbesindia.com

2. How Human-Robot collaboration will change the work environment?

As big data, analytics, and AI take over work done previously by humans, new job roles will begin to open up. These will concentrate on skills such as tracking, developing, running or designing processes that are automated.

Will you become the next Online Course Developer?

The e-learning industry is expected to hit a global market share of $300 by 2025, largely powered by technological advancements, changing business needs and a range of emerging trends in learning and growth.

1. A connected world will transform the way you work

As virtual devices allow interactions and communication in the workplace to occur anywhere, job roles and careers are increasingly redefined to fit into these boundless models at any given time.

2. A more and more global and varied pool of talent will shape job creation

Employees will become growingly multi-generational and different, while the workspace will become more flexible and active. Policies, salaries, benefits and office layouts will need to be modified to suit the needs of the new professionals.

Do you desire to be the talent management professional of the future?

Growing multi-generational workforces need a more accommodative and adaptable approach to handling and retaining talent. Each generation will have its own inspirations and methods of working, but you can't depend on stereotypes to boost productivity.

If you start developing a strong portfolio of skills now, you could become a crucial facilitator to retain and engage the diverse employees of the future, while also handling and implementing changes at the workplace.

Organizational rearrangement will change the demand for work

Organizations will be more flexible and clear, with an emphasis on project-based relationships and business sustainability. Leadership is going to play a more decisive role in the traditional hierarchical model.

Employment prospects in India

As India continues to prove itself to be a dominant force in global digital space, job roles in technology are expected to build traction as the nation's most-in-demand employment. As such Individuals require to upskill to ensure long career particularly when Robotics takes away other jobs. In the next decade, cryptocurrency, blockchain, robotics and automated vehicles – all new technologies – will become common, needing thousands of specialists.

In addition to this, space tourism offers tremendous potential and has the capacity to generate a mini-industry of tech specialists. Mission planning, experience design and launch management would have to look at from a development prism, generating thousands of jobs with specialist skill set.⍰

Although technical occupations dominate the list, it is equally important to see soft skills such as business management and customer engagement become essential, which underlines the value of human interaction at every stage of digitization.

Conclusion: While it may not be possible to predict the future course of every job at the workplace, certain competencies can help protect your future career if not present job roles. Tech and finance skills will still call the shots and simultaneously there will be a need for soft skills that cannot be automated. At the same time, education and the attitude of lifelong learning will become more crucial than ever. Education has been identified by the World Economic Forum as the number one way to prepare for the upcoming two decades of work. Though the next decade will open a multitude of jobs still the biggest challenge will be spotting people to take on the job roles.

To sum up, job seekers need a whole new range of skills to impress their prospective employers. They require future skills such as digital literacy, emotional and social intelligence for communication and problem resolution and innovation, computational thinking, and cognitive flexibility.

Chapter 10

Anytime, Anywhere and Any device – A forward-thinking concept that ensures a company's future success

Introduction – How things were before the COVID pandemic?

People used to go to workplaces, sit at the desk and perform all their work there. In the changed scenario, digitization has added a new facet to how we work. "Every day" has become "Anytime". "Here" turned into "Any place". We have already witnessed mobilization as the complete digitization of work.

The Three Strategic A's that win the endgame

Anytime, anywhere, and any device – or regarded as the 3As is not a radically new concept. This is called the ATAWAD concept – the way the world is now moving forward with this. We have been talking about this for a while now and several companies have already introduced ATAWAD in different business divisions. Organizations have equipped employees with mobile devices to access data anytime (round-the-clock) from anywhere and through any device, be it desktop, laptop, smartphone etc.,

The utility of ATAWAD concept

The ATAWAD concept aptly reflects the development of technology and the way we function. Being continuously connected is becoming just as important as the work we do. If you're at home, at a conference or in travel, you need to work together to keep in contact with others using the tools you have on hand: iPhones, laptops or computers.

A large number of millennials, who are also called as employees, convinced with the WFH option and feel that working remotely would significantly enhance their interest in specific employers. As a business model, it helps in decreasing real estate prices and overhead costs and lowers attrition rate too.

- Anytime: Digital and mobile technologies enable users to benefit from training programs during their convenient time of the day, or after office hours. This gives the agent the liberty of selecting when to focus on training programs and at their own pace. Recently conducted surveys revealed that current day's agents – primarily made up of Millenials – see the future of education as more immersive. Therefore, they are more open to concentrate on learning new things at their own pace and in their own time. ⬚

- Anywhere: Due appreciation to mobile devices and applications, training can take place at work, at home or wherever you go. This is more prevalent when combined with Massive Open Online Courses (MOOCs), which are online courses. This offers agents the convenience to access the training material from almost anywhere. More than 50% of the Millenials surveyed claim that they don't require a physical room. This makes "Anywhere" exercise a far more convincing opportunity to recruit agent officers.

- Any Device: Agents want the freedom to choose which technologies they use. With the introduction of BYOD (Bring Your Own Device), online and cloud applications are developed on mobile-optimized systems for all kinds of users. This ensures that the training program of the enterprise will be readily accessible irrespective of the device.

How people slowly evolved to resolve the COVID challenge by the ATAWAD concept? ⁇

Ever since the pandemic has engulfed our lives, it has triggered a shift in work many organizations have been forced to turn their workforce into telecommuting. As a result, different tools and technologies for business continuity and productivity maintenance have been adopted in the current scenario.

Several companies have an internal preference to use a specific application. However, their clients and other network stakeholders may have a different preference for another application.

Most companies have put in place more than one application. As per the CIO Association of India's survey, there is a tough tussle, for video conference, between Zoom and Microsoft Teams.

In a majority of instances, Google Hangouts/ Skype for Business/Meet, Skype/ and CISCO Webex have emerged as other popular choices.

Team Collaboration is one of the principal components of enabling WFH, and Slack looks like a winner, according to the CIO Association of India's survey.

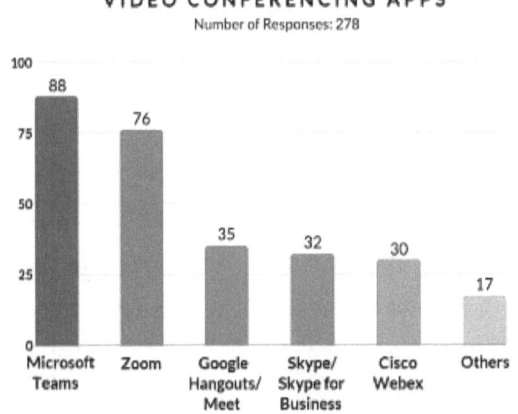

VIDEO CONFERENCING APPS
Number of Responses: 278

Source: cio.economictimes.indiatimes.com

Companies moving towards Remote jobs

Many companies today have a greater understanding of remote jobs. The benefits cover enhanced productivity and wellbeing, decreased absenteeism, greater employee development and more successful recruiting. Companies can engage the services of teams and specialists all over the world, even as they reduce overhead costs.

The job environment is evolving at an ever-greater pace, so it is important to learn and appreciate these changes. Companies can no longer afford the luxury of waiting to see what is happening. Anyone who refuses to dive would fail.

Work from home (WFH) becomes an inevitable reality

Now with COVID, no employee has dared to visit their workplace in the fear of the spread of the pandemic. So all are working from home and this concept now has become so powerful that it is going to change the world it works and the way the humans think and will bring in a total shift in the paradigm of work style. ⁇

Employees too learnt to respect the opportunity to operate remotely. Gallup, the US-based Analytics and Advisory Company, in 2017, carried out an employee management survey that revealed that the average worker was willing to settle with 8% less pay for the option to work from home.

Source: Gallup.com

Technology changes job picture

While technology has influenced the remote-work revolution, shifts in millennial-driven corporate culture and Generation G will shape the future of work. Many millennial people have been interested in technologies all their life, and they are the ones who companies should be talking about when it pertains to recruitment and retention.

Digital and technological competencies are the new sources of employment, as demand continues to show an upward trend in IT, social media, SEO and analytics, as well as new digital roles emerge in old industries such as construction, logistics and energy. Employers would have to adjust fast to what the modern generation truly wants: the freedom to function flexibly and from everywhere, greater work-life balance and more flexibility in the workplace.

The new generation working force is ambitious, creative and daring. For many of them, working and travelling at the same time – being a digital nomad – is a fantasy. Rather than taking a year's time to travel after school, Gen-Z staff will be willing to step into the job market directly, as long as they are fit to travel regularly. We are now living in an ever-connected environment, and they are many fascinating countries and hubs around the world that have adopted remote work.

How can Human Resource Development promote this development?

HR can make three key contributions. First, it can take up workforce transformation as the top of its work agenda. A business transition can become successful only when a company can shift its workforce qualitatively and qualitatively to support growth. It's something that needs to be built carefully, much like technology. Second, HR can gain experience and educate management about what they do and how they do it.

Third, it can strategically strengthen leadership and organizational culture and push the requisite cultural improvement in workplace conduct. It is supposed to make organizations and working staff more competitive and efficient.

However, this juggling act can only be accomplished and sustained if you rely on four similarly reliable pillars: trust-based management, flexible work conditions and safe and readily accessible co-working.

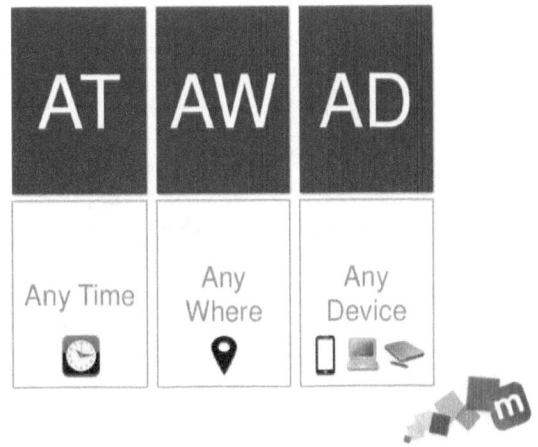

Source: Slideshare.net

Source:
https://wisembly.com/en/blog/2015/10/15/anyti
me-anywhere-any-device-the-atawad-concept

The five trends shaping the future of work

Source: /www.ie.edu/insights/articles/

1. New behaviours

A decade ago, had anyone suggested that you should learn, display, and experience all this knowledge about yourself in public, you might have thought they were nuts. Now look at where we are: we are much more relaxed leading more public lives, creating communities, connecting, interacting, engaging, gaining information, and influencing our personal experiences.

All these new behaviours are cascading through companies, and are pushing them to make improvements.

2. Technologies

Robots, Big data, the Internet of things, the cloud, automation, collaboration platforms, video, and other technologies are transforming the way we function and live.

The cloud places the power of technology in the hands of employees; robots and machines push us to reconsider the tasks that humans should and can perform. Big data gives us a peep into how we function and how customers negotiate with us; and collaboration platforms bring our citizens and knowledge together anywhere, at any time and on any device.

3. Millennials in the work environment

Approximately 50% of the population is predicted to make up millennials by 2020 and this is estimated to be 75% by 2025. The interesting thing about millennials is not that they may introduce different strategies, concepts, beliefs or working models, but that there would be too many of them.

In all respects, these are going to be the biggest group ever to join the workplace. This is a generation of technology-driven workers who can spend a longer time at home before they come across a company they truly want to work with.

4. Mobility

Today, it doesn't matter where you are based when it comes to your ability to do your job.

As long as you can connect with the Internet, there is a possibility that you will meet the same people and get information as though you were operating in the same house. We're linked anywhere and everywhere we travel, whether it's 35,000 feet in the air or a coffee shop.

5. Globalization

Essentially, this is the willingness of organizations to operate in an environment where boundaries cease to exist. The world is now more like a major community. The language you're spoken, the currency you're dealing with, and your location basis are beginning to matter less relevant.

Conclusion: The digital transition is likely to last longer and the industry needs to adjust to change!

The 3As is today's revolution, one that will transform the industry into a customer-centric, ubiquitous force.

Also, employees ought to create a daily schedule and ensure that they spend their time wisely, stay productive and remain well. Achieving these objectives involves selecting the best location to operate on a given day or the right place to focus on a specific assignment. It means taking care not to work extra time while also remaining focused.

*****

Concluding Remarks

This book gives a summary on the whole gamut of Future of work themes covering various aspects including "The New Future of Work in a Post-pandemic World", " Why modern India needs to welcome co-working/Reimagining the Future of Workspaces", " How Technology will Change the Future of Work", "Leadership in Crisis and role of the leader in reskilling Era/The Evolution of Leadership", "Preparing your organization for new employment methods", "Four C's – Creativity, Collaboration and Communication", " Virtual Pieces of Trainings Learning and developments", " The re-working of work-skills for future jobs" and " Jobs that emerge over the next decade", " This is how the future works: Anytime, Anywhere, and Any Device".⬚

As the world of work becomes increasingly complex, diverse and uncertain, traditional models of working are beginning to give way to more flexible forms of organization and employment. Technologies, globalization, as well as changing demographics of the workforce and skills gap add to the challenges facing organizations.

The objective of this book is to illustrate in practical detail how companies can operate in this new paradigm. The main goal of this book is to lend support to HR professionals and organizations they work for this journey. This is a book about how the workforce of the future will engage them, how managers will lead, and what companies of the future will look like.

The Future of the work will help:

- Stay forward in the competition
- Build better leaders
- Gain new skills
- Attract and Retain Top Talent
- Embrace flexible working environments
- Make workforce adapt to future technology skills
- Build an organization for the future
- Help employees increase the employability factor

I am sure the collection of thought pieces will be useful to budding HR practitioners in developing a set of principles that define good practice and professionalism.

This book provides a roadmap for what leaders across contexts require to do to generate high-quality jobs and develop competitive and profitable businesses.

I am hopeful that my guiding principles will help organizations embrace them to challenge outdated, traditional ideologies and practises, thereby enabling them to become more innovative, flexible and aware of the future.

=0=0==0=0=0=0=0==0=0==

- Reema Nakra